small worlds

A FRESHWATER POND

Adam Hibbert

CRABTREE
Publishing Company

Crabtree Publishing Company

PMB 16A, 350 Fifth Avenue
Suite 3308
New York, NY 10118

612 Welland Avenue
St. Catherines
Ontario L2M 5V6

Co-ordinating editor: Ellen Rodger
Commissioning editor: Anne O'Daly
Editor: Clare Oliver
Designer: Joan Curtis
Picture researcher: Christine Lalla
Consultant: Staff of the Natural History Museum, London

Illustrator: Peter Bull

Photographs: Jan van de Kam/Bruce Coleman Limited, front and back cover, pp 3, 5; Uwe Walz GDT/Bruce Coleman Limited p 4; Nigel Blake/Bruce Coleman Limited p 6; Kim Taylor/Bruce Coleman Limited pp 8t, 10, 11, 13, 19, 21; Geoff Dore/Bruce Coleman Limited p 9; Hans Reinhard/Bruce Coleman Limited p 15t; Andrew J Purcell/Bruce Coleman Limited p 18b; Jane Burton/Bruce Coleman Limited pp 18t, 22t, 29t; Felix Labhardt/Bruce Coleman Limited p 25; CC Lockwood/Bruce Coleman Limited p 27b; S Nielsen/Bruce Coleman Limited, front cover, p 28; Corbis Images pp 1, 7tl, 7tr, 8m, 12m, 14, 15b, 16, 17t, 17b, 20, 23, 24, 26, 27t, 29b, 31b; NHPA p 12t; Harry Smith Horticultural Collection p 22m, 30t.

Created and produced by
The Brown Reference Group plc

First edition 1999
10 9 8 7 6 5 4 3

Copyright © 1999 The Brown Reference Group plc

CATALOGING-IN-PUBLICATION DATA

Hibbert, Adam, 1968-
  A freshwater pond / Adam Hibbert. — 1st ed.
  p. cm. — (Small worlds)
  Includes index.
  SUMMARY: Describes the different kinds of plant and animal life that can be found in freshwater ponds.
  ISBN 0-7787-0133-6 (rlb)
  ISBN 0-7787-0147-6 (pbk.)
  1. Pond ecology—Juvenile literature. 2. Pond animals—Habitat—Juvenile literature. 3. Ponds—Juvenile literature. [1. Pond ecology. 2. Ecology.] I. Title. II. Series: Small worlds.
  QH541.5.P63 H535 1999
  577.63'6—dc21

LC 98-51710
CIP
AC

Printed in Singapore

ISBN 0-7787-0147-6

Contents

Ponds around the world

The axolotl lives in Mexico. Its cousin, the mudpuppy, is found in North American ponds and streams.

There are freshwater ponds all over the world, except at the Poles. In this book, you will visit a North American pond and see what lives there.

Most ponds are formed where rainwater has filled natural dips in the land. Some are made by people, to add charm to a landscape.

Thousands of creatures live their whole lives in one pond; others just visit in search of food or water. Ponds are small self-contained worlds. All the classes of life in ponds rely on each other for food, oxygen, and shelter. Tiny **bacteria** help the pond to support life, while large predators keep the population in check.

The leaves on these pond lilies are about the size of dinner plates. In the tropical Amazon, South America, lilies grow leaves up to two yards (1.8 m) across.

4

Pond life

Ponds are more fragile than lakes. They are shallow and small, so water temperatures can swing up or down by 20 degrees in a single day.

Pond life has to be able to survive if the pond should dry to a soggy patch of mud in the heat of the summer. It must also cope when a layer of ice seals the pond off from the air in winter.

Ponds also need a good mix of minerals and oxygen in the water. If the pond water was absolutely pure and clean, nothing could live there.

Plant life

Plants give the fish and other animals of the pond air to breathe and food to eat. Plants rotting at the bottom of the pond make good hunting grounds, while trees on the bank protect the pond from sudden changes in temperature.

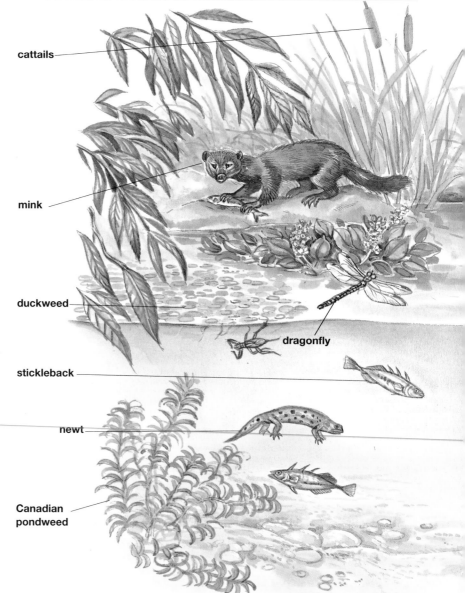

cattails

mink

duckweed

dragonfly

stickleback

newt

Canadian pondweed

Creepers and crawlers

From the tiny water flea to the great diving beetle, nearly half of the 25 major types of bug in the world live in ponds. Most feed on **algae** and plants, but the biggest insects eat tadpoles and small fish.

Big eaters

Fish, frogs, turtles, and snakes are too big for other pond animals to eat but make good meals for roaming **predators**, such as the heron. Of all pond life, the bigger animals vary the most from pond to pond.

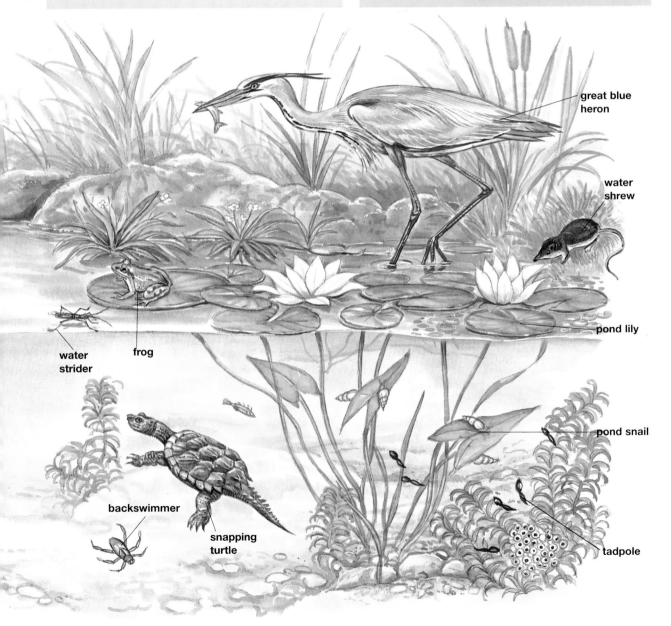

great blue heron

water shrew

pond lily

water strider

frog

pond snail

backswimmer

snapping turtle

tadpole

Plant life

Ponds contain some of the simplest plants on the planet. They are also home to complex, bug-eating plants.

▲ *The water fern looks similar to duckweed most of the year, until fall, when it turns bright red.*

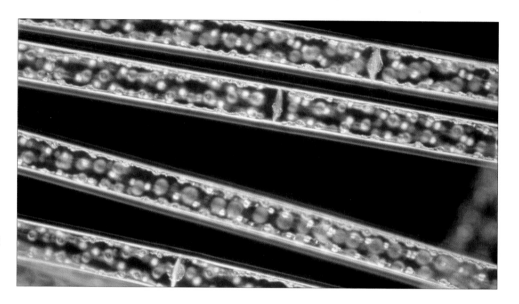

▶ *These algae, spirogyra, form long strands, just one cell thick. The strands make slimy green clumps, known as pond scum.*

A cup of pond water contains over a billion bacteria. Bacteria sometimes make a pond stink of rotten eggs because they give off a smelly gas as they break down old leaves in the water.

▶ *Rushes and reeds surround the pond. The water gets its color from millions of tiny green algae.*

The smallest plants
Microscopic plants, such as volvox, are really groups of algae. Working as a team, the algae gather energy from sunlight to make food. They become a highly efficient food factory.

8

▲ Under the microscope, volvox looks like spiky, see-through green balls. The young algae rattle around inside each little globe.

Tiny floaters

Duckweed floats across ponds. Its leaves make a bright green carpet across the pond. This carpet of leaves is an excellent hunting ground for big bugs, such as backswimmers. The duckweed's tiny roots dangle from the leaves into the water to gather minerals that help it grow.

FANTASTIC FACTS

● The smallest, rootless duckweed has the world's smallest flowers.

● Duckweed leaves have air-filled pockets that act like water wings.

● Plants such as the hornwort have underwater flowers.

● Lily leaves have a waxed surface to repel water.

Leafy weeds

Simple rooted plants thrive at the edges of a pond and in its depths. These plants, such as Canadian waterweed and the hornwort, live completely under the water and have finely divided leaves. The plants that put out leaves on the pond's surface usually have broad, flat leaves instead.

Gotcha!

Unlike most plants, the bladderwort is a meat eater! It dangles small traps, called bladders, from its feathery leaves into the water. When pond insects swim past, the bladderwort's trap snaps open, sucking in its prey. The plant digests its catch to get extra nutrients.

▲ *The bladderwort is a plant that eats insects. It sucks water fleas into its pockets, or bladders.*

Pond lilies

The pond lily has large round leaves, which push up through the water in a tight roll. At the surface, the leaves unfurl, pushing other plants aside. The surface of the lily's leaf is smooth and waxy, but the underside, where snails graze and lay their eggs, is slimy.

Lilies produce spectacular flowers, which only open on sunny days. The flowers do not open if it is raining. Rain would fill the flower and make the plant sink.

▼ *The pond lily's thick leaves make a sturdy resting place for frogs.*

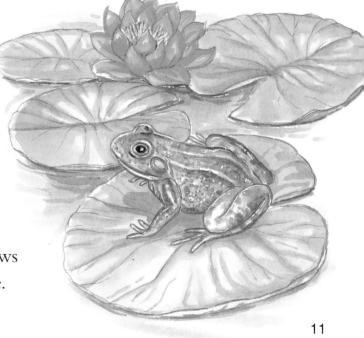

Reed or rush?

Unlike lilies, reeds and rushes grow their leaves above water. Reeds have long, flat leaves, while rushes have spikier ones. Reeds can grow in meadows as well as at the pond edge.

Creepers and crawlers

Ponds are home to hundreds of strange bugs. Some bugs slither, some swim, and some are jet-propelled!

▲ The wandering water snail has a tightly coiled shell. It lives in slow rivers as well as ponds.

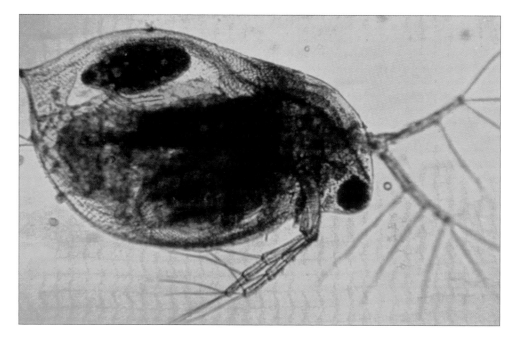

▶ Water fleas are crustaceans, which means that they belong to the same family as crabs.

One of the most useful bugs in any pond is the water flea, or daphnia, although it is only the size of a poppy seed. It uses its feelers as flippers to push itself through the water, as it gobbles up algae and keeps the pond water clear. The water flea is also a meal for most of the smaller pond creatures.

▶ Cover your arms and legs when you visit a pond—ponds are a favorite haunt of biting insects, such as mosquitoes.

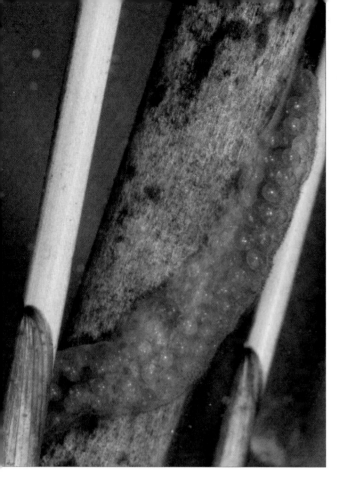

All kinds of shells

Snails eat algae, too. Some pond snails have to breathe at the surface, travelling up plant stems for gulps of air. The great pond snail floats upside-down at the surface and eats pond lilies. Most freshwater snails are **hermaphrodites**. Each adult has both male and female reproductive parts, so all snails can lay eggs.

Relatives of sea shells can also be found in pond mud. The fingernail clam filters the water for edible scraps. Fingernail clams sometimes grab the toes of a passing toad or newt to hitch a ride—which makes the **amphibians** look like they are wearing jewelry!

▲ Pond snails fix their hundreds of eggs to a stem, in a protective bag of gel.

▼ Flatworms are meat eaters: they even manage to eat small tadpoles.

Slithery worms

Worms live in the mud. They eat rotting plant materials and each other! Red worms and flatworms are easiest to see, at just under half an inch (1.3 cm) long.

Slimy vampires

Leeches are slimy worms with a bad reputation, but not all of them are blood-suckers. They spend most of their time under rocks and in the mud at the bottom of the pond, and some eat smaller worms. Blood-sucking leeches grow fat on a single meal and then take up to six months to digest it.

Bloodsuckers are attracted by splashing—so wear boots if you go wading.

Grubs in the mud

Early in the year, the pond is full of insect **larvae**. Many flying insects such as mosquitoes and dragonflies spend their youth as larvae in ponds. Mosquito larvae dangle upside-down from the surface to breathe. A sudden ripple sends them wriggling to the bottom.

Tiny midge larvae come in many shapes and colors, from the bright, red bloodworm, which swims like a snake, to phantoms, which are see-through larvae that jerk away when disturbed. Both grubs live in tiny ponds and puddles, where fewer predators lurk.

The bloodworm is a midge larva, which makes a home for itself in the mud.

A freshwater pond

▶ *The great diving beetle larva uses its pincers to stab prey.*

Killer grubs

The mud at the bottom of the pond is full of large predators. Dragonfly and diving beetle larvae are the most dangerous of them all, growing up to two inches (5 cm) long. Both have large pincers for grabbing other larvae, tadpoles, and even the occasional small fish. The dragonfly larva has a spiked lower lip, called a mask, which it can use to snatch its prey.

Little squirts

Dragonfly larvae spend up to three years fattening up in the pond, before emerging for a brief summer as flying adults, to mate and lay eggs. The damselfly larva breathes through three feathery gills; the dragonfly larva sucks water into its rectum to breathe. Though strange, this doubles as a getaway plan as the larva can squirt the water out to make a jet-propelled escape from a predator!

FANTASTIC FACTS

● Backswimmers can stab a human finger. The bite is not poisonous—but it really hurts!

● Backswimmers naturally float; water boatmen have to swim to the surface.

● Mayflies live three years as a larva but only a few hours as adults.

A sting in the tail?

Water scorpions are not related to the poison-tailed desert scorpion. Their long tails are breathing tubes, which the animal attaches to the surface as it waits for prey to come near its claws. It uses its short beak to eat tadpoles or tiny fish.

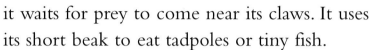

The water scorpion doesn't have to stay at the surface for air. It often hunts in the mud at the bottom of the pond, too.

Row, row, row the boat

Water boatmen and backswimmers look like beetles, but they are bugs. Instead of jaws they have pointed beaks. The water boatman uses its beak to vacuum through the **silt** on the pond bottom. The backswimmer has a sharp beak, which it uses to stab surface prey from below.

The backswimmer swims on its back. Like its cousin, the water boatman, it uses its two feathery legs to push through the water, just as a rower in a boat uses a pair of oars.

Springtails group together in "rafts" that look like a cloud of ash floating on the water.

Spring into action

Springtails look like tiny gray-black flecks, which sometimes gather on the pond's surface. They graze on very tiny pieces of vegetable matter on the pond's surface. They provide a nice source of food for small carnivores, such as young frogs and toads. A flick of their "spring" tails can propel them an inch or two into the air—a mighty leap for an insect that is only a sixteenth of an inch (0.16 cm) long.

Beetling about

Adult great diving beetles are strong swimmers and fierce hunters. Like their larvae, they have pincer jaws for grappling small fish and other prey. As they dive, they carry air in the hairs on their **abdomen** and under their wing cases. The air helps the beetles rise back to the surface.

The great diving beetle can be up to one and a half inches (3.8 cm) long.

The great silver beetle is another big beetle with its own water wings. It gets its name from the silvery bubble of air it carries. Unlike the great diving beetle, the great silver eats only plants, as an adult, at least. Its larvae are meat-eating predators that can crunch through a snail's shell.

Walking on water

Surface tension happens when a liquid, like water, meets a gas, like air. It acts as an elastic skin on the surface of the pond.

Surface tension is not strong enough to support bigger animals, such as newts. The stretchy skin does let small, light creatures, such as water striders and swamp spiders, walk on the surface of the water without getting their feet wet.

Water striders will eat any wriggling animal they can catch on the pond's surface. The insects pinpoint their prey using their four back feet, which pick up any ripples on the pond.

The swamp spider is just under two inches (5 cm) across (legs included). It has a poisonous bite.

Hunting habits

The swamp spider also uses the pond's surface tension to detect its prey. It sits with its forelegs dangling on the water surface. When it detects the wriggling of its prey, it lunges into the water, gathers the prey into its jaws, and drags it back onto its perch to eat.

Split vision

The whirligig beetle lives on the surface of the pond. It spins around at high speed in search of food. It keeps an eye out for danger, too. Both of its eyes are split in two. The top halves look for threats from above, so the beetle can dive into the water to hide. The bottom pair keep watch below, and if danger looms, the beetle flies to safety.

Pond show-offs

When it is time for a dragonfly larva to leave the pond, it crawls up a stalk, where an amazing change takes place. After a few hours, an adult dragonfly wriggles out of its old body and unfurls two brand-new pairs of wings.

FANTASTIC FACTS

● Dragonflies can fly at speeds of nearly 18 mph (29 km/h).

● The largest prehistoric insect was a dragonfly with a two-foot (0.6-m) wingspan. It lived 300 million years ago.

● Dragonfly adults mate in mid-air.

Darners and skimmers

There are two different families of dragonfly: darners and skimmers. Darners hover for long periods over their territory, scanning for prey, and have long, thin abdomens. Skimmers are stubbier. They prefer to rest on a look-out point (a twig or a leaf), then dart out to snatch food or defend their patch. Both eat all sorts of flying insects, from midges and mosquitoes right up to honey bees.

Spot the difference

Damselflies are often mistaken for dragonflies. It's easiest to tell them apart when they rest: only the damselfly tucks in its wings daintily. The damselfly's wings are rounder, too, and its eyes are farther apart and they bulge. But both species lay their eggs in the water, where the larvae, or **nymphs**, will live. The female cannot get her wings wet, so she lowers her tail as far down a pond plant's stem as she can reach, then lays her eggs inside.

▼ *Only the female green darner is green. The male's body is electric blue. Dragonflies keep their wings in flight-position even when they are resting.*

Big eaters

Big animals rarely live in a pond all year round, but some hunters stop by for a snack, and frogs and toads return to mate.

▲ From the moment tadpoles hatch, they must fend for themselves.

▶ The male stickleback guards its nest until the eggs inside hatch.

Ponds in the wild cannot support very big fish. Anything much larger than a minnow or stickleback would soon eat up all the other creatures. The stickleback has tough spines in the fin along its spine that protect it from enemies. At mating time, the male turns red and attacks any other red thing in its territory. It builds a nest for the female to lay her eggs in and looks after them until they hatch, fanning fresh water onto them.

▶ Northern water snakes like to bask on rocks or overhanging branches. They slip into the water to escape danger. They can also give off a powerful skunk-like smell to put off predators.

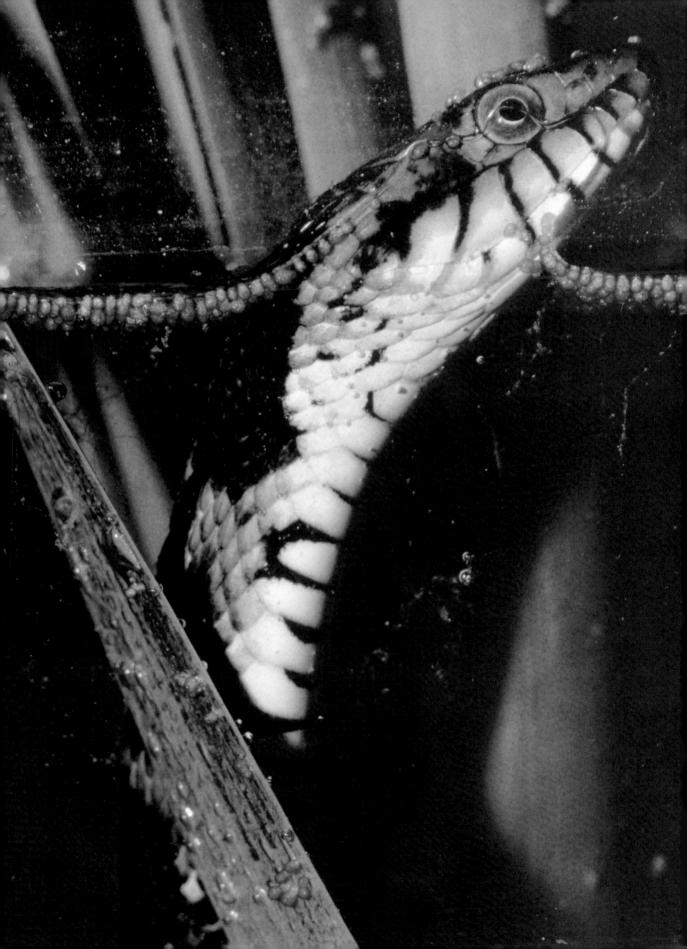

- Tadpole means "toad head" in Old English.

- Toads can lay strings of eggs up to two yards (1.8 m) long.

- American bullfrog tadpoles can take three years to develop.

Spring is here

Frogs and toads arrive at the pond in spring to mate and **spawn**. Frogs are noisiest when they are courting. The special stretchy sacs around the males' vocal cords can make a range of calls to attract a mate. Frogs' eggs form large slimy clumps, which can contain a mixture of eggs from many different females.

Under attack

Very few of the thousands of tadpoles in each pond become adults. Tadpoles are easy prey for hundreds of other creatures, including the bigger insect larvae, swamp spiders, fish, turtles, and even birds.

The American green frog returns to the pond to mate. It keeps damp in the muddy shallows.

Hop it!

The tadpoles that do grow up into frogs and toads leave the pond to find a safe, damp spot, where there are plenty of bugs to eat. They do not go far, because all amphibians need to keep their skins moist to help them breathe. Some only return to their ponds to breed, although some frogs risk being ice-bound and stay in the pond through the winter.

▲ *This common toad will spend the winter on land.*

It's a frog's life

Amphibians lay thousands of eggs with a black center and a see-through, jelly-like coating (1). The tadpoles hatch from the egg and swim by wriggling their tails. They have **gills**, and at first they look like baby fish, but with rounder bodies (2).

By early summer the tadpoles have sprouted back legs and webbed feet (3), and soon after they grow forelegs and shed their tails. Now they are like miniature adults. In a few months they are ready to mate (4), and the cycle begins again.

1

2

3

4

Toads with tails

Newts are amphibians, like frogs and toads. The main difference is that newts keep their tails as adults. They attract mates underwater, with fancy displays of tail-wagging from the male. Female newts lay one egg at a time, often taking great care to hide each one in a folded leaf. Their tadpoles keep their gills long after the first legs appear.

Newts eat insects, worms, and tadpoles—sometimes even their own!

▲ *The red-spotted newt lives on land as an adult but comes back to the pond to breed.*

FANTASTIC FACTS

● Newts swim by wriggling their bodies, like fish.

● Mudpuppies have been caught 120 feet (36.5 m) deep in the Great Lakes.

● The smooth softshell turtle can outrun a man on level ground.

Faithful pup

The mudpuppy is a strange relative of the salamander that never loses its gills because it never leaves the water. Unlike other amphibians, it guards its eggs until they hatch. The mudpuppy is found in lakes and rivers as well as ponds. It prefers muddy, weed-choked water, where there are plenty of places for the mudpuppy to hide.

Turtles are reptiles. This stinkpot has just hatched, using a special egg tooth that drops off when its job is done. Stinkpots get their name from the smell they release when frightened.

Kicking up a stink

Many types of turtle live in and around freshwater ponds. Most prefer muddy shallows where they can reach air with their nostrils.

Stinkpot turtles rarely grow above six inches (15.2 cm) long, but the common snapping turtle belongs to a different family and grows to three times that size. Snapping turtles will eat small pond animals, including birds, as well as plants and algae. Soft-shelled turtles have fleshy lips, which cover their beaks, and a tube-shaped nose, which they use like a snorkel.

The shell of a snapping turtle is soft, so the turtle relies on its strong, sharp beak for self-defense.

FANTASTIC FACTS

- Herons have special feathers called powder down that make talc, for grooming.

- The great blue heron has a six-foot (1.8-m) wingspan.

- Ermine (a type of weasel) turn white in the fall to make them invisible against the winter snow.

Patient hunters

Herons visit quiet ponds, where they stand still for hours waiting for a meal to come within striking distance of their long, sharp bills. They stab underwater for fish and also pick off frogs and toads. Their long necks distinguish them from other birds. Herons are the only birds to fly with their neck bent back and their heads tucked between their shoulders.

▼ *The great blue heron will feed whole fish to its brood of hungry chicks.*

Silvery swimmer

The water shrew is one of the few **mammals** that spends its whole life by one pond. It burrows into the banks, hunting underwater by day and night for tadpoles, insect larvae, and worms. Shrews are tiny. The American water shrew can walk on water, just like a water strider.

Underwater, the water shrew looks silver. Bubbles of air trapped in its fur give it a silvery sheen.

Furry and fearsome

Mink are much larger than shrews. They gobble up bigger prey, including fish, mice, frogs, snakes, salamanders, bird eggs, and small water birds or chicks. Their feet are partly webbed to help them swim through the water. Mink are especially good at catching muskrats, often making their dens in the muskrat burrows. They are hunted by foxes and sometimes owls, but their biggest enemy is food shortages. Minks mate between January and March and give birth to a litter of around four kits (babies) a month later.

Mink kits feed on their mother's milk for six weeks. After that, they must hunt on land and in water.

Your own pond

You do not have to find a pond in the wild to enjoy pond life.

▶ *Is there an ornamental pond near where you live? Most people stock their ponds with goldfish, which eat other pond creatures. You can still find water fleas and plant life.*

Some pond life will come and find *you*, if you collect some rainwater in an old pail or bucket. Just leave the water standing outside for more than a week in the summer, and you will begin to notice the pond life arriving.

Scoop a glass full of water from your bucket. You will find that the water looks greenish. That is because algae has moved in, and if you are lucky you may see dark green strands of spirogyra threading through the water. If you used a bigger container, such as an old bath tub, water striders flying past will drop in to eat the insects that get trapped on the surface.

After a little while, midges and mosquitoes will leave tiny wriggling larvae

▶ *When you see these mosquito larvae dangling from the surface, look out for their hungry parents!*

in the water … if you do not want to get bitten, now might be the time to pour out your bucket pond and go looking for the real thing!

Words to know

abdomen The rear part of an insect's body.

algae Very simple plants.

amphibian An animal that lives both on land and in water.

bacteria A type of single-celled life-form.

gill A feathery organ used for breathing underwater.

hermaphrodite An animal with male and female parts.

larva An immature insect.

mammals Warm-blooded, hairy animals that suckle their young.

nymph The larva of certain insects, such as the dragonfly.

predator An animal that hunts other animals for food.

reptile A cold-blooded, scaly, air-breathing animal.

silt Fine, underwater mud.

spawn A mass of frog, toad, or fish eggs.

Index